YOUR ANGELS HEALING WORDS TO GUIDE

A SPIRITUAL LIFE BOOK OF MEDITATION AND AWAKENING

BY ANDREW MARMION R.P.N, B.A. DIVINITY
MINDFULNESS DIP S.N.H.S.

The ANGEL FELLA

YOUR ANGELS HEALING WORDS TO GUIDE

A SPIRITUAL LIFE BOOK OF MEDITATION AND AWAKENING

BY ANDREW MARMION R.P.N, B.A. DIVINITY (HONS)

MINDFULNESS DIP S.N.H.S.

BOOK ONE

THE ANGELIC GUIDANCE SERIES

SECOND EDITION

Dedicated to all those who love their angels and those who support my work and buy my books. God Bless.

TABLE OF CONTENTS

Introduction

I always wanted to make an angel card deck of my own, and the angels heard my request. They inspired me to write poetic verses intuitively, and I was blown away by the result. This book is comprised of some of those verses, and, to help you focus on them better, I added little reflections and prayers after each one.

I hope that you will experience the loving guidance of the angels through the use of these little meditations. I certainly feel them close when I use them. Allow their poetic nature to take you to the depths of solace and peace. Let the angels touch you at your deepest centre and find healing and renewed purpose for your life.

Likewise, these meditations will help you get closer to your angels and feel them closer to you. Yes, they'll serve to help you get to know your angels better no matter if this angelic relationship is new to you, or if you're already familiar with them in your daily life.

How to Use this Book

I'm just writing this section to suggest a 'how-to' approach concerning the angelic meditations. But, you can ignore this section if you're used to such works, meditation, and the like. However, I know there's bound to be a lot of less sure people, so here's a simple way of getting the most out of this book.

1. Sit comfortably (or lie down if you're sure you won't fall asleep!) in a dimly lit room with a candle burning and a holy picture or image before you. I like to use an angel statue. I can focus on it if my mind is wandering a lot.

2. You can have some gentle music playing in the background if you think it will help. I generally use one from YouTube. There's loads of music to choose from, too.

3. Greet your guardian angels, and ask them to help you relax while doing this exercise. Ask them to work in your mind and calm your body, to bring you the necessary healing you need for the day.

4. Next, breathe in as deeply as you can through your nose and exhale through your mouth. Count to four as you inhale and again as you exhale. Be aware of the air going in and out and your chest rising and falling (This is a simple Mindfulness Technique). Do this for a few minutes or until you feel centred.

5. Read the little angel poem you've chosen to use. Read it slowly two or three times. Does anything jump out at you? Maybe a particular word or phrase resonates with you. Perhaps it helps conjure up an image of some sort. If so, repeat it slowly several times and ask the angels to help you understand why it's so meaningful to you.

6. Talk with your angels about what you're experiencing. Don't worry if you find it hard to concentrate or that your mind wanders a lot. It doesn't matter too much as long as you're doing your best. Sometimes I just sit and be aware of my angel's presence. I focus solely on this and have a little chat with them. And sometimes that's enough. You can also use the reflection and prayer provided with each meditation if you think that will help.

7. When you have finished, thank your angels for their help and the time spent with you. The angels never ask us to thank them, but I always believe it's essential to do so. It's good for us to show a little humility and gratitude.

If you practice this often, it will not be long before you are aware of your angels during the day. Your awareness will expand as your intuition takes over. This angel connection will also help you experience them, and feel them with you.

I love it when the angels make themselves known. One way they've done this is by playing with my hair. I can feel them patting me on the head at times and tickling me, too. It can be both funny and annoying, depending on when they're doing it!

Don't worry, though, when you don't have that experience of the angelic presence. That's normal too. It's more important to know they are there, to be aware of it. Experiencing their presence – well, that's a bonus.

When I lose that sense of the angels' presence, I don't worry about it. Let's face it; we're human and have to live our lives in this world. It's too hard to function normally with the head constantly in the clouds.

Likewise, not feeling the angels close tests our faith. That's one way we grow spiritually. It speaks volumes to them when we go on talking to them, continue to have them in our lives, even when things are not going our way. It also lets the angels know we value their help and are grateful to them. At such times, they are closer and more attentive to our needs – they are actually carrying us.

And know this. The angels will not be happy for you to stay focused on them. They point the way to God from whom they come. They are creatures of God just as we are, and their primary role is to lead us to God while protecting, comforting, and guiding us. We can talk to them as we would a friend, but they are not to be worshipped. That privilege belongs to God alone.

Ultimately, the angels want us to practice God's presence since He is our creator and, as such, is our beginning and end. It's Him to whom we return at life's end, to live eternally in His presence – a presence of infinite holiness, love, and goodness, where all our needs are met, our ultimate healing is realized.

Being with God, we will want for nothing and will live in constant joy and ecstasy, which grows in intensity since we've entered eternity, for there is no end to God or His many attributes. So it makes sense to ask the angels to help us practice the presence of God. But they'll be happy enough for us to practice their presence, to begin with as, in the long run, they'll use that to help focus us on God.

Anyhoo! Enough of that for now. Please find the angelic meditations below and enjoy them. And feel free to make prayer cards out of them – to carry them with you, stick them on the fridge, share them with friends and family. Whatever you fancy.

Meditations

Here are the angelic meditations below. Take your time and have a read through them. I hope you enjoy using them and grow in love for God and the angels. Remember, it's not all business either. They want you to have fun with them too!

Angelic Diplomacy

Bonds are easily broken, though repair can maintain.

Is it enough though to sustain, when hurt has occurred,

When pain is in sight and easily framed?

Is it better to be right or happy, to dig in the heels,

Or see the other's point of view?

Reflection: Think about how important it is to be open-minded to other people's points of view. When we do this with compassion and understanding, it releases us from fear, and we can allow others to believe what they want without needing to manipulate or influence them. This keeps us free of fear and from being drained of our energy.

Prayer: Angels of light, who work for the higher good of all in times of mutual disagreement or misunderstanding, we surrender our fear and ego so that we can listen freely to others and allow them to have their own point of view. Thank you that your intervention keeps me free of fear and any need I may feel to manipulate or control others. Amen, and it is so!

MUSICAL ANGELS

Can you hear the music, sense the divine?

It calls to you from Heaven's columns, its halls of joy.

Can you hear their harmony, see resounding smiles as they play

Their instruments to touch and heal?

Can you play their music, make such angelic sounds?

Can you? Can you...?

Reflection: Love is musical, and love begets love. What do I do to pass on love, to help others awaken to its beautiful music? Do I have a sense of the angels working in my life? Do I identify with love's music and accept it from others in my life, including my angels and God?

Are there blockages in my life to giving and receiving love from others, including God and His angels? If so, what can I do about this?

Prayer: Dear angels. Give me a heart that is attentive to love's ways. Open my mind and heart so that I may both give and receive love freely and without fear. Angels of light, help me identify any blockages so that I may be freed of them by you. Amen, and it is so!

Dancing Angels

Beckon the angels come forth and be not afraid.

It gives them joy to be near you and to serve.

To hear your invitation makes them dance with grace, good cheer.

Their dear one has answered, said Yes to Heaven's request.

And now they're here dancing, and forever to stay with us at rest.

Reflection: Think about what it means to have your guardian angels in your life. Think of how happy it makes them when you invite them to be with you each day. See them dance around you with joy, eager to help guide and guard you, comfort, and support you along life's journey.

Remember, they're with us always and rejoice as they see us grow in love for God and each other.

Prayer: My dear angels, thank you for being near me each day to guide and guard me. Thank you for being of service to me in so many love-filled ways. Continue to remind me of your love as I go forth to be of service to others. Amen, and it is so!

Nature's Angels

Friends of Mother Earth kissed and caressed by nature's vibrant arms.

See them that cheer and encourage nature's growth, entering auras willing to embrace.

They whisper lovingly, see each blade of grass grow strong, delight in flowers: red, white, and gold.

At this nature's angels sound their harps, instruct nature to resound in our souls.

Reflection: The nature angels care for God's creation with the utmost care. They encourage its growth and tend it when sleeping at year's end. They never leave God's creation and are ever eager to share its beauty with us.

The nature angels also play a part in nudging us to pay attention to the beauty of nature and to reflect on where it comes from and how it gives freely to us, like our guardian angels, without expecting anything in return.

Prayer: Angels of nature, thank you for inviting us to share more deeply in nature's embrace. Ever remind us to respect this great gift of God, which gives of its fruit freely and without any expectations. May I, too, mirror beauty and love in my dealings with others, especially concerning those who need to be uplifted and healed this day. Amen, and it is so!

ANGEL WINGS

You are never without support, my friend,

Never without wings that lend a shadow to protect

From rays, bright and broad, seeking to blind you.

These wings enfold, also protect you in the dark,

Lighten the shades that speak coldly to your heart.

They shelter you from tricks of the mind,

Seeking to seduce you from an angel's path learned,

That which leads to life, and new life's spark!

Reflection: The angels guide and support us through the myriad of life experiences, both those which draw us closer to God and those seeking to divert us from the spiritual path. The angels lead us to the truth so that we might follow ever onwards to experience the glory of God and his heavenly kingdom. They shield us in many ways, and we are often unaware of how effectively they do their job.

Prayer: Holy angels, thank you for guiding us along the spiritual path. Protect us now and always from any negativity or evil which seeks to deviate us from the path of God's love. Thank you for the many times you have protected us mentally, physically, emotionally, and spiritually, especially on those occasions when we have been unaware of this. Bring us safely home to Heaven's shores, dear angels. Amen, and it is so!

Friendly Hands

Angel hands are made for holding; angel hands are hands
that care.

They stroke and touch us gently remind that to us they are
always near.

A grieving heart they seek to heal and a cheery heart rejoice
in its ways.

Laughing, they laugh with us, when troubles looms the
coming storm they shoulder strong.

They're friends who never leave or abandon, so entrust
yourself to their loyal care.

Reflection: Our angels are attentive to our every need, even those of which we are not always aware. Their unconditional love means they cannot but help, heal, and nurture us. They take part in our lives and are interested in the choices we make and in the smallest things that happen to us.

Our angels are even interested in what clothes we pick out for the day, the food we eat, the music we listen to, and to those whom we're chatting. They are the most intimate of friends and always seek out our highest good.

Prayer: I am so glad, dear angels, that you take part in every aspect of my life. Please continue to be there for me through thick and thin. Remind me often that you are by my side so I may smile and nod in recognition of this and with gratitude. Amen, and it is so!

GOODNESS

Goodness is my name, a reminder from whom I came,

So call on me for decisions needing to be made.

When your head says, "I will," but your heart says, "no,"
instead,

Then confusion of choice opens you to divisive thoughts,

Its scatty actions and harmful ways.

But remember, dear soul, Goodness who is near,

Can help you with your mind's true point of view.

Reflection: The angels help us seek inner unity, peace of mind, and heart, for if we are not at peace with ourselves, how can we expect to be at peace with others? So then, when our heads and hearts are at odds, remember to ask your angels' help for inner resolution and peace. Go forward with confidence that they hear your call and are working for your highest good.

Prayer: Angels of goodness and unity, may we be always of one mind and heart in the service of God and each other. Since we cannot do this well without peace or integrity, chase from us all confusion and discord that seeks to divide our inner being. Thank you for doing this and helping us choose the way of goodness. Amen, and it is so!

LISTEN

Listen to your angels with ears open wide.

Be eager to hear their words, encouraging, so dear.

Be not afraid, dear soul, they whisper soft and sweetly clear.

Lean your head on their shoulders strong, and offer a silent prayer.

One of love and gratitude, one that Heaven loves to hear.

Reflection: Listening to our angels' guidance is of great importance. It's advisable to adopt this listening practice, especially during times of prayer and meditation. This helps us to be more attentive, so we recognise solutions when they come to us.

Quite often, angelic nudges and guidance can be a moment of recognition, an Aha! moment. This can happen in so many ways, e.gs. Through people, we meet on a particular day, something we are reading, or song lyrics to which we're listening. Be prepared for this recognition by the heart as your intuition reassures you that you are hearing your angels aright.

Prayer: Teach me, my angels, to listen for your loving words of encouragement; open my mind and heart to your gentle prods. Please open my life to your constant support and love as you help me recognize the solutions to life's challenges to learn the lessons of life well.

Thank you, my angels, for your patience when I don't listen well or respond in a way that is for my highest good. And thank you for your constant support, which is ever strong and sure. Amen, and it is so!

HAPPY FEET

I walk this world but never alone, my footsteps guided by
Heaven's light.

If I lose my way, it's not for long as I see those wings
surround footfall's path.

This gentle presence provides a sense, relief that I may know,

That shadows of those angel wings

Assure my happy feet of paths well travelled and worn.

Reflection: God's angels are a reflection of Himself. Just as
He loves us unconditionally, so do they. They are sent by God
to journey with us until we reach our heavenly home.

They lead us along paths that guide us there and they are
quick to steer us back to the way of goodness when we
wander from it, though they will not interfere with our free
will.

Prayer: Thank you, angels, that your presence reminds us of
God's love and that, like Him, you are there to help us when
we wander or stray and bring us back to Heaven's pathway. I
choose that path now and always. In my mind's eye, I smile
as I see Heaven's shores. Amen, and it is so!

Innocence

Innocence, a sweet touch that protects the heart, keeps the soul untainted and true.

Without guile, and like a child's heart, the everlasting light of love passes through.

Open your heart to the beauty of love and close the rear door to resentment's hate.

This ensures that insidious spite will never be your life's fate.

Forgiveness is needed, love's nurturing touch, to knead away the knots of bitterness and pain.

Yes, open your heart to a touch of love, experience innocence, and the peace of its ways.

Reflection: Innocence is an angelic quality that we have too. However, it can be affected by the difficulties and pain of life experiences. The angels ever remind us of our heavenly calling and always invite us to return to that innocence, which can never be truly lost.

What does this mean for you? What do you need to change to realise your innocence again? Do you need to apologise to anyone? Do you need to let go of unnecessary fears or clinging bonds of overdependence or addiction? Allow your angels to help you with this. It can be surprising what crops up.

Prayer: Thank you, holy angels, that I am called to innocence like you. When anything should muddy my soul's bright hue, help me clear it so that my innocence is restored, and I can celebrate life more fully as a child of God.

May I recognise with your help those areas in my life where I need forgiveness and healing. With you, I release this muddy yuck! And choose the way of innocence and love. Amen, and it is so!

PEACEFUL SPIRIT

A peaceful spirit is a joy-filled soul, the fruit of willingness to give God your all.

A peaceful spirit holds hands with God's will, accepts life's happenings, smiles at it all.

A peaceful spirit knows his Lord's voice and in His presence peacefully stands.

A peaceful spirit knows God's love is awesome, and His gifts abundant and clear.

A peaceful spirit waits for His action, trusts that He is near.

Reflection: Do I lack peace in my life? Is it because I'm living a distracted or selfish existence instead of one of love and service? What can I do today to encourage peace to enter my life ever more fully? What action need I take, or is it more a case of waiting on God?

I can also ask my angels to help me identify what it is I need to do to restore peace lost or to deepen it. Perhaps I need to pray and meditate more often. Maybe I need to alter my pace of life.

Prayer: I pray today for a peaceful spirit ever aware that God is always near and that I rest secure in His love and mercy. Holy angels, help me realise that peace is a gift of God and that it serves me well to remain at peace with myself, life's happenings, others, and God. Thank you for your peaceful embrace. Amen, and it is so!

ABUNDANT FRUIT

God has two hands like you or me, but they can't contain the
weight of His love.

His abundance escapes through the palms of His hands,
finding its way to receiving souls.

God's generosity is an answer to prayer, freely given it fills
souls with His care.

His abundance is more giving than the asking ever is,

For God's glory won't stop how His love it outpours.

Reflection: God's loving abundance is overflowing because
His love is eternal. He is always pouring His love into hearts
that are ready to receive it. There is no better door through
which it will enter than by loving and generous hearts.

Likewise, the more we give, the more we receive. Dare we
open our hearts to receive this loving abundance from God?
Dare we share it with others, even with those whom we think
don't deserve it?

Prayer: Thank you, God, for your loving abundance. Open my
heart to receive it in my life, particularly that of your
blessings, love, and kindness.

Holy angels help me and remind me to be loving and
generous towards others even when, at times, it may be

inconvenient. And may I adopt an attitude of compassionate service, including those who are challenging to be around. Amen, and it is so!

PARTY ANGELS

If angels had bodies they'd enjoy life's comforts too.

They'd laugh and feast and feel no guilt in the least.

The angels encourage us to party, have fun,

Take advantage of life before it's long gone.

Rejoice in life and celebrations invited to,

Being part of humanity, it's the way we're meant to.

Reflection: Have you ever thought that your angels are thrilled to see you enjoying life, whether it's a holiday abroad, celebrating a birthday, or having a quiet cuppa with a friend or two? Are you ever aware of them at such times? Do you ever picture them before you – smiling, glad to see you happy?

Some people experience guilt when taking time to enjoy themselves, but this is a necessary part of self-care. It's how we recharge the batteries and keep that bounce to our step. If you feel guilty concerning this, ask yourself why you are feeling that way. Perhaps it stems from needing to be needed, over-giving, or unnecessarily taking on others' responsibilities.

Prayer: Thank you, dear angels, for being with me during fun times. Thank you for encouraging me to enjoy myself and be with friends and family. Help me release any fear or guilt I may have concerning taking time to relax or be with friends. I take charge now and allow you to transmute those thoughts and feelings to those which serve my highest good. Amen, and it is so!

Glory Gained

Angel hearts rejoice this day as listening souls come their way.

Open ears they treasure with joy, ever ready their tasks to employ.

Eager to help, eager to share, they lend us God's glory, which shines everywhere.

They help us to seek it in all we think, say, and do, that we mirror the likeness of God's glory too.

Reflection: The angels wait for us to ask them for help. And it's important to ask as they will not interfere with our free will.

They want to shine the light of God's glory on us so that others recognise us as spiritual beings who are attentive to God's ways. In this way, our loving actions will also shine forth for others to see. Hopefully, this will help them recognise that they are loved and supported, too. Perhaps, they will then be more willing to help others in their daily lives. And so, God's glory will shine ever onward as we all recognise the need for compassion and love.

Will we see that glory shine forth in our world, or will we keep ourselves to ourselves?

Prayer: Thank you, my angels, for your constant help. Thank you for shining the light of God's glory everywhere, particularly in my direction. I pray that I reflect God's love and light to others in all that I do and say each day to bring them comfort and happiness. Amen, and it is so!

Goals Achieved

Life awakens dreams hidden in the mists of time.

Breathing on that mist, the angels its treasures reveal.

See the dreams offered you, the goals to be achieved,

Choices, possibilities, nothing's ever written in stone.

Choose heart's true desires and you will own your goals.

Worked out, blessed as hands are put to the plough,

Motivation is given by dreams realised now.

Reflection: We all have dreams and aspirations concerning our lives. But our experience can impede us through fear, and worry can erode our goals. That's one of the paradoxes of life.

Let us ask our angels to encourage us to explore our gifts and dreams, no matter where we're at in life. This may take time and effort, but if we persevere, we can realise our dreams. And dreams that come to fruition result in a grateful heart.

Prayer: Dear angels, awaken the passion for life's dreams in my heart. Help me discover my life purpose and make my dreams a reality so that I may have a greater sense of being and have true happiness in life. Amen. And it is so!

HIDDEN JOY

Joy is yours, it's yours to keep, a gift for the soul, inner and true.

Joy is a witness of God's loving presence, echoing, it's resounding in you.

We angels are immersed in joy and share it with your soul,

A shining hidden gift, but to be shared with all.

Reflection: Having joy in our lives is what makes life worth living. But joy also reflects the presence of God to the world through us. It's hidden in the sense that people don't tap into spiritual joy, the deepest and eternal aspect of this gift.

Most tend to drift along just living with finite joy that accompanies living a material life only. Much energy is wasted and expended by such people who need to continually renew these experiences to keep this superficial happiness in their lives. Let us not be such people.

Real joy, however, is spiritual and comes from our deepest being. We need not waste time and energy to keep it there as it's not dependent on the material. Likewise, it's not something we're meant to keep to ourselves; we're to share it with all those we meet.

But perhaps people will ask why we're happy first. It is then we can share our reasons why. Through our witness, they too may come to accept and live a deeper spiritual life.

Prayer: Thank you, holy angels, for bringing the gift of God's joy to me and implanting it in my heart. I choose joy now and always, even when life proves challenging or seems unfair. I share it with all my brothers and sisters, too, fellow children of God.

May my joy help lift the hearts of those suffering so they may know they are cared for and loved. May the spiritually barren discover, through my spiritual joy and happiness, their need for God and His love. Amen, and it is so!

DREAM ANGELS

Our sleeping hours are real in all dimensions,

There is no place where dreams do not reach.

But an angel's care moulds and guides them, to give them meaning, the intent is to heal.

They whisper 'Hush!' when tempests threaten to provide illusions for the soul,

And wait to welcome finite time to eternity where each and all are real.

Reflection: How aware are you that your angels participate in your dreams? Dreams are the bridge between Heaven and earth; they open a door where eternity meets finite time and space. Dream angels can help mould our dreams, too, so we derive more meaning from them and gain more profound healing.

Perhaps you've experienced Deja vu from your dreams. What does this mean for you? Or maybe you have repetitive dreams? This could be your angels tapping your subconscious, asking you to pay attention to an aspect of life needing to be addressed.

Maybe you have dreams to warn or guide you concerning one of life's issues. Perhaps you have dreams needing to be shared with others. Many dreams are meaningful, so pay heed to them and keep a dream journal when you think this would be helpful.

Prayer: Thank you, my dear guardian angels, for protecting me in my sleep. Thank you for guiding my dreams and that eternity meets me in finite time and space during my sleeping hours. May I find true meaning in my dreams and so be blessed with peace and healing. Amen, and it is so!

PLEASE SEE NEXT PAGE BELOW

I hope you have enjoyed this little book and recommend it to friends and family. Please leave a review with Amazon as it helps the ranking and so reaches more peopleThanks.

May the holy angels always be with you and yours, and bring you light, happiness and healing. Amen. May it be so!

Please find an excerpt of *Angelic Thinking* below, the next book in The Angel Guidance Series. The introduction gives a juicy explanation as to what the book is all about. Another wee freebie for you all. Enjoy!

Introduction

Have you ever considered that angels exist? I imagine you have or you wouldn't be reading this book. But here's another thought to consider. Do you believe the angels love us enough to care what we're thinking? Do they care what thought patterns we develop?

This book addresses the negative and destructive thought patterns which affect our emotions, behaviour, and our lives. Ones which have developed over time can be identified and, if asked, the angels can help us be rid of them. Simultaneously, they help us replace them with healthy thought patterns.

Obviously, there is leg work involved on our part, but we don't walk this journey alone. Our angels are there to guide and protect us through the process. This involves them affirming, confirming, comforting, and healing us. Their loving reassurance leads us forward to an abundance of emotional and psychological freedom. This, in turn, leads us to experience the true freedom of the children of God.

This process takes time and effort, but the rewards far outweigh the former, and the results begin to occur speedily. My mum used to say, "Son, God gives you the spade, but you do the digging." How true that is. Thankfully, though, I'd like to add: the angels help us know how much digging to do, where to dig, how deep to dig, and where to put the dirt. In other words, we're not handed the spade and told to get on with it while God and his angels twiddle their thumbs, halos, and whatever else they fancy.

This book is also founded on the sound principles of neuroscience I studied as a psychiatric nurse. Additionally, the spiritual aspects contained in these pages have helped shape and bring this book to life. In other words, the content of this book wasn't plucked out of the ether and shaped into some kind of candy floss. It's solid stuff used to help you identify the areas of thinking you need to change and of which to be healed.

The angelic material helps to direct it and makes it more meaningful to the spiritual person, enabling the receiver to change and become more like God. After all, that's what the angels want for us – to become more like God.

It is hoped that you too, in turn, will be a light-bearer to those around you. Seeing you change, and being aware of the healing love you manifest as a result, it is my belief you will help others take advantage of the opportunity to change, grow, and heal, too.

So, read on, dear friends, and enjoy putting into practice what you find in these pages.

Chapter 1.
The Story of My Thinking

I don't want this book to be all about me. It's about you, but, what can I say? I have a story of my own and telling some of it will help set the scene for what follows. So, please, bear with me.

I was born and brought up in Glasgow, Scotland, but had a difficult childhood in many ways. I survived sexual abuse by a neighbour as a child, and by a doctor when I was a youth. And just a little side note. If anyone thinks that you can't be healed of childhood abuse, that's not true. I'm living proof that you can not only survive and be healed of child abuse, you can also thrive. I'll repeat that:

YOU CAN ALSO THRIVE!!!

The Gollum Years

Nothing, absolutely nothing is impossible for the angels to heal at God's behest. I suffered for years from depression because of so many childhood issues. I was also diagnosed with Post Traumatic Stress Disorder and God alone knows what else. I've forgotten. I was seeing psychiatrists, psychologists, and counsellors for years. Although they did their best to help me they couldn't block out the past and how it had affected me. Additionally, I found it extremely difficult to let go of it. It clung to me and affected me in so many ways.

Despite this, I had spiritual experiences as a teenager and tended to think of it as God's way of making up for my crappy childhood. My giftedness was interrupted though because of the toxic thinking traits which infected me like a merciless disease. I was shaped and moulded into one with a victim mentality, one who hid and isolated himself a lot, but this was to change. And thank God it did.

In the meantime, I experimented a great deal with alcohol and, to a lesser extent, drugs. I also used copious amounts of food and television to block out the pain, numb my emotions, and help me live in the real world. I experienced reality as something unbearable – not just challenging. I was depressed and suicidal at the age of nineteen, and only God knows why I didn't kill myself.

God intervened on such occasions, and I would find relief, but the hardest period of my youth was definitely between the ages of nineteen to twenty-one. I was suicidal every day and used to repeatedly bang my head off the wall to try and stop the pain. Imagine the psychological pain I was in if I thought such unhealthy, drastic actions would help. Loneliness and despair were my constant companions at this time, but I didn't tell anyone how I felt. I didn't think they would care, and at that time, I didn't know anything about depression or the available treatment for it.

Mind you in the '80s, there wasn't as much emphasis on counselling and psychotherapy as there is now. Likewise, there's far less stigma concerning depression and other mental health issues. Thankfully, professions such as psychotherapy are more readily accepted and are available to help increasing numbers of people. I believe the angels have played a part in this development – God recognising the need we have of this and our willingness now to receive it.

I would describe my years of early adulthood as the 'Gollum Years'. Gollum, you know, that gangly grey creature in Lord of the Rings, he was consumed by the power of the One Ring. He coveted it so much that he called it My Precious. That's how I viewed copious amounts of alcohol, endless T.V. viewing, and masses of junk food. Oh, and don't forget the unending stream of cigarettes. They were all so precious to me!

If you've seen the film, you'll know that Gollum hid way up in the Misty Mountains to be alone with the ring where it tortured and changed him beyond all recognition. The same happened to me. I hid under a drunken haze in front of the television screen or was stuffing my face. That was my reality. How sad.

But I don't look back at that person with disgust; neither do I judge him. When the time was right for me, divine timing, I was to leave all that behind me, one step at a time. I still struggle with binge eating occasionally (at the time of writing this book), but I know that too is being healed. And this is what this book is about: God's healing through how and what we think.

Physically, Gollum turned grey and lost his hair. Mentally, he became deranged and murderous (he previously murdered his best friend for the ring). He talked with the ring as though it were a real friend. Spiritually, he was left bankrupt and in a state of despair. He both loved and despised the ring. That was also true of me. I both loved and detested the grip alcohol and food had on me. I also felt like such a slob spending hours watching T.V. What a waste of my life.

Needless to say, my thought life was diseased. I was at dis-ease with myself. Thoughts of self-hatred were common, as was the dark mist of poor self-esteem and lack of self-worth. There was no sense of self-acceptance or confidence, and I was still depressed and intermittently suicidal. I could see no way out, no light at the end of the proverbial tunnel.

Time marched on though and, with several divine and angelic interventions, I realised my giftedness again. As I gradually woke up to the futility of my existence, I reached out for help. When I did so, the angels were there ready to respond. Several kind people were put in my way. Other support came from books and tapes, and I also went to spiritual places and connected a lot with nature. Gradually, oh, so gradually, I changed for the better. I received so much help and healing to live my life's purpose: to be happy and to help others through my work with the angels.

THE VICTIM MENTALITY

My thinking, though, was still affected a great deal by the victim mentality. This way of thinking is common in today's society, and it certainly had me by the throat at that time. Poor me dominated my thinking. Life was so unfair and mistreated me. It also resulted in a passive way of living, as though waiting for something, life (anything!) to change. But it was my attitude and way of thinking that needed to change. And this was to change concerning me, others, and God.

I knew the victim mentality was associated with my childhood issues and that I was still affected by them. Don't

get me wrong. I had tried several counsellors who helped –
but only to a certain extent. I just could not shake the poor
me attitude.

I did not realise it at the time, but my toxic thinking was very
much connected with my immature emotional life: it was
very much linked to the pain of the past. In other words, I
was living my emotional past in the present, so much so, if
somebody hurt or challenged me, I would experience the
pain in a much exaggerated way and go into crisis mode! I
became exhausted from these repeated reactions, and
ensuing dips in my mood, and became a psycho-emotional
prisoner. Thankfully, I was to realise I was the jailer, so I had
the keys to my own prison cell.

Practising the Mental Cleansing and Refurbishment Exercise
has genuinely helped a lot with this. This practice is the main
content of this book, which will bring you so much healing, as
it has me. Pretty soon after beginning this daily exercise, I
began to experience my self-worth, while self-acceptance and
healthy self-love dawned on the horizon. My self-talk became
more positive, and the way I related to myself and others
improved as a result.

Several years previously, I had stopped drinking alcohol, quit
smoking (over 30 cigarettes a day), and I stopped watching
so much T.V. This had helped me tremendously – but this
mental cleansing...wow!

More pieces of the puzzle emerged when the angels entered
my life with more insistence. It was either that or I had
enough healing achieved to enable me to listen. Either way,
as I responded to the angels, I began to learn so much about
myself. I also saw how much I was loved and how the angels

wanted me to be like them: to love unconditionally, and to serve others.

Don't get me wrong. I'm not there yet, not by any means, but I'm trying, and I know it will be a lifelong lesson. But it's the journey that's important. I can leave the concern of the journey's end to God's good grace.

The last piece of the puzzle was put in place when I participated in a unique hosting of the 7 Archangels. I invited the archangels to my house for a week (asked to do so by a friend). I prayed for their help while they were with me. The heaviness that remained to me left me; the depression and difficulty in doing everyday tasks vanished. The sense of aimlessness and despair was replaced with hope, vibrancy, and a sense of purpose.

These beautiful archangels also did something marvelous. It took a few days for me to realise it, but they had cut the cords which linked my mental pain involving past events from those which occur in the present. My past lost its grip on me in this respect, and what a relief!

A miracle had indeed happened, which allowed me to hear and see the angels better and be of service to others more freely. It also meant I was no longer worried about others hurting me. I was free to learn how to deal with hurt as it happened so I could forgive and let it go instead of nursing the pain or licking my wounds.

Just an aside here on forgiveness. I don't mean to dismiss other people's pain when I say this, but forgiveness is vital to the spiritual life and, I believe, is the biggest obstacle impeding spiritual growth. Holding onto painful wounds done to us by others feeds our festering wounds, which result in interior ugliness. It can be the beginning of a Gollum scenario as we start to resemble that which we hate.

However, even if every fibre of my being says otherwise, I use my will to forgive. I stay with the turmoil, the anger, and resentment until it subsides. I keep practicing this until I forgive that person.

And remember, forgiving someone isn't about letting them off the hook. Of course, I acknowledge I've been wronged and am hurting, but I choose to forgive to set myself free from resentment and anger, any sense of revenge that I might want to take. It's not easy to do, but I keep trying and forgive myself when I don't get it right or delay in forgiving someone.

Now, back to my little story about the archangels. After their powerful intervention, I launched into my life's purpose with a bang and a fizz of fireworks. I started reading people's angel cards with ease and accuracy. I also began drawing people's guardian angels (I love doing this). It never ceases to amaze me when I understand either a drawing's symbolic meaning, or an angel's relationship to his/her charge. And most of the time, I also know the angel's name.

I have to add that the angel I draw is not usually the primary guardian angel I make contact with: it's another. Instead, t's a guardian angel other than the one(s) who accompanies us into this world when we are born. It's as though the primary guardian angels push them forward for a bit of recognition and gratitude as they are the least recognized by us.

I believe it's important to point out that several angels usually end up accompanying us through our life's journey. Some we acquire along the way may leave us again when there's no longer a need for them, while others remain for the rest of our lives together with our primary guardian angels. Then others come and go throughout our lives; they visit whenever their help is required. I have one such angel, Simon, one of Archangel Raphael's healing angels. The thing I like about him is he's such a chatterbox, a bit like myself. He also knows how to take a compliment.

Another thing I started to do was hold angel parties in people's homes, including praying with people; amazingly, the angels began to heal them, especially emotionally. The strange thing was none of this shocked or disturbed me in any way. It all seemed to come so naturally. Admittedly, I initially thought I was a charlatan, a phony. I thought God and his angels couldn't possibly be using me. But they were, and still are to this day. I've also had so much positive feedback that I can't deny the truth of it all. It's truly a humbling experience and a great privilege to serve others in this way.

I now know I am to serve people every day until my Maker calls me home. No matter how difficult that is, I've not to shrink from the task. Like the angels, I've to approach people in a non-judgmental way and – as I said before – with unconditional love in my heart. The angels told me to be love in the heart of society. No doubt, I'll be learning to do that until I leap into eternity, but I'm happy to do it and can forgive myself for my human failings.

DEATH TO THE NIGGLIES

I love the angelic dynamism of life and think about how they operate without demanding our thanks or recognition. They work away quietly and tirelessly. Lord, the average person is annoyed at not being thanked for making a cup of tea. But the angels love unconditionally, long to serve us, and please God.

Although they don't demand our thanks, the angels are appreciative when we give it. It's one of my daily activities: to spend a few minutes thanking my angels for their presence, their love, friendship, guidance, and protection. They do so much more of what we'll never be aware of until we break through to eternity.

It's only fair if you're asking at this point, 'What's all this got to do with my thought life?' It has everything to do with it. Like me, you have thoughts and thought patterns that affect your daily lives and relationships. And, if you're honest, not all that goes on in your mind is pleasant or comfortable. Your self-talk can, at times, leave you feeling deflated, guilty, or shame-filled.

Perhaps it's worse. Do anxiety and negativity claim much of your thinking? If, like me, you want to heal your life and relationships and develop a happy and peaceful thought life, you've come to the right place. Read on and fear not; we're getting close to the nitty-gritty.

I'm finally beginning to put to death the nigglies – that's what I call negative thinking. You know, the mental tape that can switch on in the head and tell you a pack of lies about yourself, ranging from 'I'm no good', 'I'm useless' to 'Why would anyone bother with me anyway?'. You know what I'm talking about.

Every human being has an internal dialogue and it's not always pretty. The problem is, if negative thoughts are allowed entry, they can begin to grow, fester, and spread since they become lodged as unhealthy thought patterns. If more negative thought patterns are allowed to take root, this influences our daily lives and relationships in harmful ways.

Although positive thinking is a useful tool to help change this, I believe today's world needs something more. The great thing is this 'more' is based on how we learn: listening, thinking, writing, and applying. The method I adopted, and still use to this day, has helped me overcome many negative thought patterns. It has helped me heal the way I relate to myself, others, and God. This change and progress are ongoing. It's a lifetime's work (he mops the brow), and I'm glad I'm on board with it. I shudder to think of what would've happened if I hadn't taken the necessary help and made the changes, which I did. Thank God for his healing love and his angels.

The decision to put the nigglies to death was the starting point for me and, I believe, is for you too. Whether you loathe negative thinking or take some kind of twisted pleasure in it (I know I did some of the time), you will need to reach the decision that you don't want it in your life anymore.

That means you no longer get to play the victim, wine and dine with it, manipulate or control others, gossip, criticise, or blame yourself or others for life's woes. All that stuff is illusion and fear-based! Okay, life might throw us curveballs, but is it better to meet these situations with serenity or with moaning, resulting in our unhappiness? Isn't it better to see life's challenges as opportunities to grow in the love of self, others, and God? Isn't it better to be more angel-like?

In other words, you have to try and let go of all the junk, all the negative thoughts, and behaviour concerning others and past situations, for this does not serve you well. If you do let go or keep trying (I've not yet perfected this myself), the upside is that you experience so much peace and happiness, an abundance of well-being and joy. And I don't mean the fleeting kind you get from munching away at ice cream and doughnuts. I'm talking about deep and lasting spiritual happiness, which makes the good times better and the challenging times more comfortable to work through.

My thinking has changed so much that I've begun to think of difficulties/hardship as growth opportunities. It may be painful at times, but they're great opportunities to learn and mature. If you're raising an eyebrow of scepticism I have to say, 'Okay, okay.' There are times it's challenging to see it that way. Like you, I'm human and still learning, but I know I can work through the emotional storms and am confident that all will be okay, so long as I don't give in to self-pity. Dear God, that stuff's ugly and so, so painful. And do you know what? – It's so unnecessary.

Self-pity never gives. It always, always takes. And it steals. It steals peace of mind, self-worth, self-esteem, a sense of belonging, and being wanted. It tells the brooder that they're unloved, and this is such a terrible, terrible lie!

However, you have to want to change. Only you can make that decision, and I pray you do. In fact, if you're reading this right here, right now, I believe that you're ready or nearly ready and just need a nudge through the door. Your angels will help you by doing just that. They can even do it quite literally.

That reminds me of an event a few months before writing this book. I was lying in bed and had remained there longer than intended. I felt this hand grab the back of my neck and give me a good shake back and forward into my pillow. You can imagine the fright I got. No one likes being awakened by surprise, never mind in such an abrupt way.

I knew it was Samuel, one of my angels that woke me, and the way he did suited his personality. He's the most serious and masculine of all my angels, and every bit as devoted to helping and healing me. It was his way of helping me get ready to meet the day. I certainly didn't fall back to sleep after that rude awakening!!

ANGELIC TIDBITS

1. Angels help us not just to exist but to thrive!
2. Angels persevere in helping us
3. Angels lead us towards healthy self-love and self-acceptance
4. Angels delight in helping us find our life's purpose
5. Angels help us realise change is possible

If you enjoyed the first chapter and wish to purchase *Angelic Thinking*, please <u>CLICK HERE</u>.

And please leave a book review with Amazon as it helps the ranking and so reaches more people. Thanks so much

Andrew Marmion lives in the West of Ireland. He helps people find meaning and healing in their lives through his books and angel coaching. For more information please visit his website at <u>www.andymarmion.com</u> He also invites you to join his Facebook group where you'll meet some amazing people. Type in The Angel Fella: Angels Hangout.